The Prophecy
The Process
&
The Promise

There is purpose in every step of your journey

Wanda R. Presberry

Wanda R. Presberry

The Prophecy, The Process and The Promise
There is Purpose in Every Step of Your Journey

Book Cover by: Info@innomarkgroup.com

Editing & Formatting by: Pieces of Me Publications, LLC
Number: 419-322-0438
Email: pom@piecesofmepublications.com
Website: www.piecesofmepublications.com

Dedication

I dedicate this piece of work to my husband Aaron and my daughter Casey who are always pushing me to go on. My husband, my rock who helps to keep me grounded and is so supportive and to my daughter who is always there and never misses a beat. Thank you for loving and encouraging me the way that you do. I also dedicate this work to my mother who is forever showing me love and support in whatever I am trying to accomplish. I love you Mama.

Wanda R. Presberry

Table of Contents

Acknowledgement 5

Purpose.. 6

Praise for 7

Foreword 8

Introduction 9

Chapter 1 16

Chapter 2 23

Chapter 3 29

Chapter 4 34

Chapter 5 37

Chapter 6 53

Chapter 7 57

Chapter 8 61

Chapter 9 71

Chapter 10 83

Chapter 11 87

Appendix 90

Conclusion 91

About The Author 92

References 93

Acknowledgement

Thanks to my Pastor and Bishop, Dr. Pat McKinstry, for being everything that you are to me. I cannot thank you enough for your love, your support, your encouragement and your correction. You have taught me, whatever I do in life to do it with the spirit of excellence. You have shown me this is possible because you lead by example.

Thank you Dr. McKinstry, for your devotion to who God has called you to be, for the love that you have shown God's people and all those you encounter, and for showing me what falling in love with "this great Gospel" looks like. I have come to know Christ even more through you. I am and will be forever grateful for this divine connection that has pushed me in my purpose and is causing me to walk in my destiny. God bless you, Bishop McKinstry for the ground you have toiled, the seeds you have planted, and the trees you have nurtured.

Purpose

The purpose of this book is to investigate and highlight key aspects of the process by which God uses to bring us into our promise. Its focus is to enlighten us with practical thinking and the word of God. Its goal is to gain a better understanding of what makes each of our journeys unique and the process we must endure is tailor made for us as individuals. Every one of our stories are different, but at one time or another we must all be "processed out" of our trials, our difficult situations and even our circumstances.

It is my personal belief, that when it pertains to becoming a part of and committing to the body of Christ, we have a choice. We can choose a life of love and righteousness with Christ or we can choose to fight against it. A life on the run is no life at all; running from what is right and holy, running from the calling God has placed on your life and running from your destiny will undoubtedly become a life of misery.

~Wanda R. Presberry

Praise for The Prophecy, The Process and The Promise

"The Prophecy, The Process & The Promise" is a must read for the believer in Christ Jesus. This book is written to encourage the believer in Christ Jesus to endure the time that is between the Prophecy they have received and the manifestation of that promise. In this book Elder Presberry addresses the frustration and discouragement that often follows a prophecy. She walks you through and motivates you continually throughout the book. Her analogy of the grape in the wine press and the firing of the pottery clay opened my eyes to how I was feeling in the midst of my personal "Process". After reading this book, I felt empowered to keep the faith, to keep my head held high and to trust the process. If you are looking for a book to inspire and uplift you on your journey I recommend you read this one.

~Minister, Carolyn Hobbs

Foreword

Those times when you are like *"LORD what is going on?!"...* or when you feel like you are at the end of your wits. What about the time when you know *"This is IT... "I've hit ROCK BOTTOM!" Those times!* These are the type of situations that author Dr. Wanda R. Presberry is speaking of when she explains how God takes us through a process to get us to our promise in her captivating book entitled "THE PROPHECY, THE PROCESS AND THE PROMISE." Dr. Presberry takes us on a journey thru the vicissitudes of life while comparing and contrasting the examples and how people in scripture handled the circumstances and promises of God. She does this and at the same time reminds us that the process that we go through is designed specifically for us out of God's divine wisdom and omniscience emanating from His immeasurable LOVE FOR YOU. If you have questioned God, or lacked clarity of how to handle the pressures of this life, or even needed guidance on how to advise others on the difficulties we inevitable face in life - the book is a treasure!

~Elder, Tina Lawrence

Introduction

The purpose of this book is to open our eyes and to remind many of us about the prerequisite to receiving the promises of God. When we say, yes to the promise we say, yes to the process, and whatever that may entail. Process is present in every area and at every stage of life. When we begin to count the cost, we get a better picture of what the journey will look like. When we consider the cost our expectations change, we begin to expect a challenge.

Therefore, we have a better chance at arming ourselves for the fight. Nothing good in life comes easy. Sometimes there is a struggle and it takes some long-suffering to get through. Even Jesus on His journey asked the Lord to let this bitter cup pass.

Matthew 26:39, *And he went a little further, and fell on his face, and prayed, saying, O my Father, if it be possible, let this cup pass from me: nevertheless, not as I will, but as thou wilt.*

We also see that He ended up accepting the will of the Father. He had to go through the process. It was necessary. It is important that we approach the things of God with a realistic view. It is not always easy, and there may be work to do, but with Christ we can and will be victorious!

"FOR GOD SO LOVED THE WORLD…"

The Ultimate Prophecy:

For God so loved the world! Jesus Christ had one of the most alarming assignments in history! The plan of salvation was laid out before Him and He accepted the challenge. We cannot begin to look at the promises God has for us as individuals without examining the process by which they are obtained. In light of doing this, we must first consider the promise of salvation and the process that Christ had to endure in order to bring the promise to pass. To overlook the One who made the ultimate promise and all other promises possible is to overlook, or dismiss the divinity of Christ. Without the ultimate prophecy of the ultimate promise made to man, no other promises would be relevant.

Coming of Christ!

Galatians 4:4-5, *But when the fullness of the time was come, God sent forth his Son, made of woman, made under the law, to redeem them that were under the law, that we might receive the adoption of sons.*

Matthew 1:21-23, *And she [Mary] shall bring forth a son, and thou shalt call his name Jesus: for he shall save his people from their sins. Now all this was done, that it might be fulfilled which was spoken of the lord by the prophet, saying, behold a virgin shall be with child, and shall bring forth a son, and they shall call his name Emmanuel, which being interpreted is, God with us.*

2 Corinthians 5:19, *To wit, that God was in Christ, reconciling the world unto himself, not imputing their trespasses unto them; and hath committed unto us the word of reconciliation.*

Christ paid the ultimate price for a promise made to humanity. He endured a process that no man ever could, not because He had to but because of God's love for us.

John 1:14, *And the Word was made flesh, and dwelt among us, (and we beheld his glory, the glory as of the only begotten of the Father) full of grace and truth.*

In order for us to be able to receive salvation, Jesus Christ had to go through a process. He had to step out of glory and become flesh.

With all His divine power He made Himself man, became like us, experienced like us, suffered torture and death all for us to receive the promise that was prophesied by the Father. With all His power and authority, He could have fought and destroyed those who sought to take His life, but instead He gave it up willingly for us.

Matthew 26:53-54, *Thinkest thou that I cannot now pray to my Father, and he shall presently give me more than twelve legions of angels? But how then shall the scriptures be fulfilled, that thus it must be?*

Jesus was human and divine at the same time. He has two natures. He understands what it is like to suffer, to feel pain, and all types of emotions. He knows what it is like to feel alone. Matthew 27:46

declares, Jesus cried out on the cross and asked God why had He forsaken him.

There are times when we may feel alone, but we must trust that God is right there. He sees, He knows and He cares. We must trust in the quiet times that God is working on our behalf. It is in those times when we do not feel Him near we must trust Him more. Jesus knows what it feels like to want to take the alternate way out.

In Matthew 26:39 Jesus told God to "take this bitter cup from me," but then he said, "nevertheless not my will but thy will be done."

Sometimes we feel like saying, God do not let me go through this, take this from me God. However, when we realise what is at stake we can say, okay God I can take it, just help me. If this is what you want me to do, then I will do it. He was completely selfless, and many times for the sake of others we must be the same way.

For the sake of the life that God has promised to breathe into our children, our grandchildren, our family members and friends we have to hang on in there. We have to endure the process. When God chose to use you to reach others there was a task set before you.

There was a process proposed, you just did not have all the details. Had you known all that would be required of you, you may not have accepted the challenge. We want the promise without the process. The process is costly, but do we want to pay the price. We are faced with the reality of the process, then we look at the promise.

We have to decide is it worth it? I am so glad when Christ looked at the promise of salvation for you and me that He decided that it was worth it. He took it for me and He took it for you. He could have changed his mind and come down off the cross.

If Christ had chosen power and authority over humility and sacrifice we would not exist today. Christ dying on the cross was a vital part of the process that had to take place in order for the blood to be shed for the atonement of our sins. He had to be buried in order for Him to be risen. It was all a process that was too much for a mere human to withstand.

There are many gods that are worshipped, but give me the God who died for me, was buried and got up again. Give me the one who went to the cross and shed His blood for the remission of my sins. Give me the only one true and living God who has offered salvation to man. Give me that God! He was the ultimate sacrifice who paid the ultimate price and no other god could have done this.

"When we look at the promises God has spoken to us through prophecy and through his word, it is very inviting. We want every good thing He has for us, but what will we have to go through to get to it?"

Chapter One
DID I HEAR WHAT I THINK I HEARD?

Discerning the voice of God is something that is vital to a healthy relationship with God and to our spiritual growth and maturity.

Recognizing the voice of God takes training.

1 Samuel 3:1-10, *Now the boy Samuel was ministering to the Lord in the presence of Eli. And the word of the Lord was rare in those days; there was no frequent vision. At that time Eli, whose eyesight had begun to grow dim so that he could not see, was lying down in his own place. The lamp of God had not yet gone out, and Samuel was lying down in the temple of the Lord, where the ark of God was. Then the Lord called Samuel, and he said, "Here I am!" and ran to Eli and said, "Here I am, for you called me." But he said, "I did not call; lie down again." So, he went and lay down. And the Lord called again, "Samuel!" and Samuel arose and went to Eli and said, "Here I am, for you called me." But he said, "I did not call, my son; lie down again." Now Samuel did not yet know the Lord, and the word of the Lord had not yet been revealed to him. And the Lord called Samuel again the third*

time. And he arose and went to Eli and said, "Here I am, for you called me." Then Eli perceived that the Lord was calling the boy. Therefore, Eli said to Samuel, "Go, lie down, and if he calls you, you shall say, 'Speak, Lord, for your servant hears. So, Samuel went and lay down in his place. And the Lord came and stood, calling as at other times, "Samuel! Samuel!" And Samuel said, "Speak, for your servant hears."

Samuel had not learned the voice of God but he was fortunate enough to have someone in his life who could instruct him. God will place people in our lives who can teach us how to discern the voice of the Lord. God speaks to us, people speak to us, the enemy speaks to us and we even speak to ourselves.

We can never trust what the enemy says and as for people and the words we speak over our own lives, we must test them against the word of God. We must make sure the words line up with what God says in His word about us and every situation we may encounter. God's voice will only speak that which lines up with His word and we must be able to recognize when it is the voice of God and when it is not. The enemy wants us second guessing what we hear and whether what we hear is from God. God's voice will never contradict His word.

Recognizing God's voice with confidence requires practice, position and proximity.

Practice: We learn the voice of God when we practice being obedient to Him. The more we obey the voice and word of God the closer we get to Him. The more we obey, the more intimate we become with Him.

Position: Sometimes we have to sit or lay prostrate before God. Our physical position matters as much as our spiritual position.

We must have a place we can go where it is just us and God. A place free of distractions, a still quiet place where we can give Him our undivided attention.

Proximity: We must dwell and live in God's presence. Staying at God's feet, staying near Him causes us to get to know Him deeper than we can imagine. The more time we spend communing with Him the more we will recognize His voice.

John 4:13, *Jesus answered and said unto her, whosoever drinketh of this water shall thirst again; but whosoever drinketh of the water that I shall give him will never thirst; but the water that I shall give him shall be in him a well of water springing up into everlasting life.*

When we can hear God's voice, obey His word, and speak His truth, then we have reached an acceptable level of maturity. This shows we are preparing for the things He has promised us.

Discipline: We must train ourselves to hear and obey the voice of God. This brings discipline in our lives and we need it in every area.

The obvious is that we cannot follow God's voice if we do not recognize it. We must be able to distinguish the voice of God by spending as much time with him as we can. When God speaks, because the natural man cannot comprehend the spiritual we will question if it's God.

1 Corinthians 2:14, *But the natural man receiveth not the things of the Spirit of God: for they are foolishness unto him: neither can he know them, because they are spiritually discerned.*

God Speaks to our intellect/soul but He connects with our spirit, that part of Him that is in us. He is speaking to our intellect to change our thinking. Intellect is the faculty of reasoning and understanding distinguished from what one feels. When dealing with human intellect we want to avoid rationalism.

One who rationalizes usually will promote reason as the supreme authority and the answer to all life's problems. He feels that he does not need God or the Bible to tell him about the things pertaining to his life. He believes he can look within himself for the revelation of life and he further believes that he can eventually and always figure things out for himself.

Through human intellect he can overcome any problem. This is a very dangerous frame of mind to live in. It will keep us from hearing the voice of God and when hearing the voice of God, we will question what is being said and will most certainly misinterpret every time.

Questioning if God is speaking to us and what He has spoken will keep us from our purpose and our destiny and we will not be able to obtain those things he has prophesied over our lives.

1 Corinthians 2:9, *But it is written, eye hath not seen, nor ear heard, neither hath it entered into the heart of man, the things which God hath prepared for them that love him.*

We haven't seen it and cannot imagine what He has planned for us. We need to put on the mind of Christ.

1 Corinthians 1:19, *For it is written, I will destroy the wisdom of the wise and will bring to nothing the understanding of the prudent.*

He destroys our intellect and helps us to put on the mind of Christ. Our thinking is limited, and He must start with the mind in order to get the body to follow.

According to Romans 12:2, we are transformed by the renewing of the mind. When God renews our mind, we will question the voice of God less and less. We will go from asking the question "Did I hear what I think I heard?" to declaring, "thus saith the Lord!"

Nuggets of Promise:

When in doubt get quiet, be still and meditate on God's word. Every answer we need is in there. Doubt is a strategy used by the enemy to steal the word and promises of God from us. If he can cause us to doubt what we are hearing or what God is showing us, then he can keep us from receiving the word. We have to receive the word in order for it to take root within us. So be quiet, be still and listen for the voice of God. He will speak it again.

Chapter Two
THE WORD OF GOD SPOKEN IN OUR LIVES

When the word of God is spoken in our lives we must allow it to take root. Every word we hear is a seed and if it is a good seed we must let it take root. We must water it and nurture it until we see it spring forth. When we hear the word, we must receive it and put it into action in our lives.

Luke 8:1, *Now this is the meaning of the parable: The seed is the word of God. The seeds along the path are those who hear, but the devil comes and takes away the word from their hearts, so that they may not believe and be saved....*

When we hear the word, and receive it in our hearts it will begin to produce the things of God from within. However, in order to hear the word, we must go where the word of God is being preached and taught. God is everywhere at all times. He is omnipresent. This does not mean we should only rely on hearing from him at home. Yes, he can speak to us anywhere, but there is a reason that we have churches with ordained Pastors who have been called and set in place by God

Romans 10:14, *...for, "Everyone who calls on the name of the Lord will be saved." How then can they call on the One they have not believed in? And how can they believe in the One of whom they have not heard? And how can they hear without someone to preach? And how can they preach unless they are sent? As it is written: "How beautiful are the feet of those who bring good news!" ...*

Hebrews 10:25, *let us not neglect meeting together, as some have made a habit, but let us encourage one another, and all the more as you see the Day approaching.*

There is a blessing in coming together with the saints, we are strengthened and encouraged by one another when we come together in one place.

God speaks and His words are solid and reliable. We can trust what God has said to us. God's word will not return void.

Isaiah 55:11, *So shall my word be that goeth forth out of my mouth: it shall not return unto me void, but it shall accomplish that which I please, and it shall prosper in the thing whereto I sent it.*

John 6:63, *It is the spirit that quickeneth; the flesh profiteth nothing: the words that I speak unto you, they are spirit, and they are life.*

When God speaks a word into our lives it is given so that we may live. He speaks life to the dead things in us to cause them to grow and that which He does not want to grow he cuts it away with His word.

When God sends His word into our hearts He is watering that which was planted in us before we were even born.

Jeremiah 1:5, *Before I formed thee in the belly I knew thee; and before thou camest forth out of the womb I sanctified thee, and I ordained thee a prophet unto the nations.*

That means God knows everything you are and He knows who you will become. He formed you in the womb of your mother's belly. He put everything in you then that points to who He wants you to be. You were a seed planted in the womb, but you also carry a seed. There was a seed within a seed. As God waters and nurtures us, He waters and nurtures what is on the inside of us.

Once a parent gives birth to a child he does not abandon them to figure out life on their own as if their job is done. A parent never stops being concerned for their children. When a child is hurting the parent feels it. A parent loves and cares for that child until their last breath and would protect them with their very own life. That child will forever be a part of that parent.

This is how our heavenly Father feels about us. We are all His children, who were only carried by our parents. He allowed our parents to conceive us but we belong to Him. He watches over us closely, waters and nurtures us like only He can. God loves and cares for us so much that he gave His only begotten son (John 3:16.) He covers and protects us and He calls us His own. So, every word we hear from God comes from His love for us. He is always guiding us with His love. Even when He speaks a word of rebuke it is always laced with His love for us.

The word of God spoken in our lives will guide us right into our destiny. It will lead us into the things He has for us to do and the things He has for us to be. We must be obedient to His word. No matter how we get it, His preached word, the Bible, or the prophet God is using. We must be obedient to His every word.

Many times, we will hear God speaking and the challenge may not be "Did I hear what I think I heard?" The challenge may be, do I really want to do what He is telling me to do? We are faced with the urge to disobey.   Do not do it. It is not something you want to start, because the more you do it the more comfortable you become.

Disobedience eventually will cause God to discontinue all conversations. God is a gentleman He does not force himself on anyone. We have to have a made-up mind to obey the voice of God in our lives. The more we listen and do, the closer we can walk with Him.

God speaks into our lives to bring to pass the purpose of why we are here. He speaks to provoke us to be our best self in Him. He encourages us with His word so that we can encourage others and help build the Kingdom.

Nuggets of Promise:

When God speaks a word to us, we must receive that word and take it to heart. We have to believe if God said it, He will perform it. He will give us every opportunity to see it come to pass. When He speaks He is using His creative ability to make our lives what He has ordained them to be. Since God spoke it all we need to do is agree. Agree in our hearts, agree in our spirit and agree in our actions. His word is true.

Chapter Three
THE PROPHECY

Prophecy is reception and declaration of a word from the Lord through a direct prompting of the Holy Spirit and the human instrument thereof. Prophecy is for the up-building and the encouragement of the individual Christian and of the church. There was a time, early in my walk with Christ that I believed prophecy was bad news. I had heard so much emphasis placed on the "dooms day prophet" that the thought of receiving a prophecy was a little unsettling.

This is why we have to study the word of God for ourselves. Once I began to study the word I saw that not only were there prophecies of destruction to those who remained disobedient to God and would not repent. There were prophecies given that pointed to the promises of God for people as individuals and the Kingdom of God as a whole. God sends His word to build up and encourage us. He sends His word to rebuke, which if we heed His word it will restore us. He brings His word to heal and deliver. When He speaks into us we must also ask for understanding. We must be prayerful as to recognize the way and the timing in which the word is to be fulfilled.

When God speaks a word to us that points to His promise, we are the instruments that will be used to bridge the gap between the word and that promise. When we get a word from the Lord usually we get excited.

We shout, we praise, we dance, we run and sometimes we even fall out. What we need to do in the midst of all the excitement, is stop and ask God, what will it cost me? I wonder if we counted the cost would we still be all in for the blessing, all in for the miracle? Would we still be shouting and praising if we knew the journey would not be so easy? There may be opposition from every side when we decide to go after that thing God said we can have, because things that are worth having do not come easy. We may experience dark times, lonely times, stress and struggles, but we have to hold on to the word that was spoken over our life, because it is worth it all.

Oftentimes, God speaks to us and we don't fully understand what He is saying. This is a time we must follow Him closely so that we do not veer off track. When He gives us a word, soon after He will give us instruction. Our job is to heed the word spoken, and to follow the directions that will lead us directly to the promise. If we only trust God, we will see what He has promised us. Our promise is in the place that He is leading us to, in Him.

From the Bible Dictionary

The Contrast between the Promise and the Prophecy:

THE PROMISE
- Relates to what is good, desirable and that which blesses and enriches
- Ordinarily implicates the entire human race in their provisions
- Promises deliberately have a continuous fulfilment for generations
- The promise of God is unconditional
- Embraces many declarations of God

THE PROPHECY
- May contain Notes of Judgement, destruction and calamity when people and nations fail to repent
- Prophecies more typically are aimed at specific nations, cultures or people

- They invoke promise when they wish to speak to the distant future.
- Most prophecies are conditional and have a suppressed "unless" or "if" you repent attached to their predictions of judgement
- Usually directed to more specific events

Walter C. Kaiser Jr.

The Promise and plan of God, then is indeed His own word and plan, both in His persona and His works, to communicate a blessing to Israel and thereby to bless all the nations of the earth.

Nuggets of Promise:

What has God spoken to you? The prophecy that God has for your life involves your purpose in the Kingdom of God. It involves the work you will do for Christ and the means by which it will be done. We need to pray over the prophecy and ask God how to walk in what He has spoken. God is strategic and there is order in all that he will have you to do. Every step in your journey has purpose. Listen and be directed of the Lord.

Chapter Four
WHERE AM I?

Oftentimes, when we begin the journey of our process it feels very unfamiliar to us. Have you ever felt that God has you in a particular place but you cannot explain it? It may feel as though you are in a particular place and at the same time you cannot identify the place that you are in. This is a place of transition. We have been here before but for some reason it feels different each time. There are many different periods of transition that we will experience in life, but the transition that ushers us into the process of getting us to our greatest victory can be the most challenging.

We transition in and out of relationships, on the job, starting school, having children, experiencing significant financial gain, or loss etc. When we die we transition from this life to the next. Transition is a phase of life that is ever present. It can be a time of chaos and it be a time of peace. However, it happens with us it is a time that calls for seeking God like never before.

When we are in this uneasy and unfamiliar part of our journey we have to be very careful that we guard our minds and our hearts.

If we are not careful we will begin to have anxiety and fear will set in. We must stay focused and stay prayerful throughout the entire process. In fact, we can do that right now.

Prayer for the process:

Father in the name of Jesus, I pray for the person reading this right now. I lift them up to you God. No matter what situation they are in God touch them right now. Take away fear and anxiety and replace it with your peace that surpasses all understanding. Cause them to fully trust in you. Allow them to travel through this unfamiliar territory with courage, taking authority over everything that is not like you. Strengthen them for the journey and shine a light in the path of their process. In Jesus' mighty name, Amen.

Nuggets of promise:

There will be quiet and dark times in our process when we cannot see what God is doing. We may sense in the Spirit that something is going on, but we just do not know what it is. In times like this we have to trust God and keep moving. God is staging your, "What is next?" It is like being at a stage play, it is the end of scene one, the lights go down and the set starts changing in the dark.

You cannot see what is happening, but you know that there is movement. You are waiting on the lights to come back on so you can see how the set has changed. You are waiting with anticipation to see, what is next? Right now, at this stage of the journey the lights are down low, you cannot see where you are at, but trust me, there is movement. Just wait and see what God has been doing. Wait and see what is next?

Chapter Five
THE PROCESS

God takes us through a process to get us to our promise. The process is a time where we are being tried, we are being transformed (our character), and we are being prepared. We are developed through testing, trying and most of all through timing. Joseph went through a tough process. He had to endure many things in order to see the prophecy come to pass which would save his family. He was betrayed by his brothers, sold as a slave and put in prison.

All this time Joseph was being tried. God used each situation and maneuvered him throughout the whole process to get him to his promise. He was being guided by what seemed to be impossible situations to a divine position of authority. Some of you through your impossible situations are being elevated to divine positions of authority! This is the process that leads to promotion! This new position of authority gave Joseph direct success to what God had promised him. It was prophesied that through him his family would be saved from famine in the land, but Joseph did not count the cost. He did not know what it would take for him to get what God had promised.

The process that we go through is designed specifically for us. The phrase "What doesn't kill us makes us stronger' is so true. There are times when the pressures of life, all its challenges seem to come upon us all at once, and it seems too much to bear. Have you ever been at a place where there was one thing after another happening? Well, I have! All I remember thinking is, this must be God because the devil cannot fight this good! Of course, I laughed about it but in all actuality, I was going through my very own process.

Everything is not the enemy. Sometimes it is God processing us and getting us ready for the blessing. When God is getting us ready He sends us through processing. I am picturing an automobile on an assembly line, and God, Jesus and the Holy Spirit are the assemblers. They start with the foundation, then they add the motor, the most vital parts, then they do the cosmetics, and finally they add the finishing touches.

In our process not only does God add things to us, but He strips us of those things that will not be useful for where He is taking us. God has to prune us. He has to cut away those things that will not bring forth fruit. He cuts away desires, habits, even old mindsets, anything that keeps us bound and keeps us from moving forward in the things of God.

John 15:1-2, *I am the true vine, and my Father is the farmer. Every branch in me that bears not fruit he takes away: and every branch that bears fruit, he purges it, that it may bring forth more fruit.*

When this is done, just like a tree, we bear more fruit, we look better and we reach higher heights. When God does the pruning, our potential is greater. Like a skilful surgeon, He uses His scalpel which is the word of God and cuts things away from us that we don't need.

Hebrews 4:12, *For the word of God is quick, and powerful, and sharper than any twoedged sword, piercing even to the dividing asunder of soul and spirit, and of the joints and marrow, and is a discerner of the thoughts and intents of the heart.*

We are changed in our process. We are conditioned not only to exist but to thrive in the environment and atmosphere He has ordained for us. The level He is taking us to is too high an altitude for dead weight. We must be able to soar without extra baggage.

There is pain in the process and this pain causes all types of feelings to surface.

- Nobody understands what I am going through.

Jesus understands what you are going through and so do others. Nobody understands more than Jesus Christ himself. He endured the beating, the shame and the cross and He had to experience it alone. That was His walk. That was His journey. It was in the purpose and the plan that God had for His life.

- Feeling Confused - I do not understand why this is happening

For times of confusion we need the peace of God. Philippians 4:7 declares, *And the peace of God, which passeth all understanding, shall keep your heats and your minds through Christ Jesus.*

- Frustrated - Nothing seems to be working out right.

God will dry up every resource we think we have in order for Him to be magnified, in order for us to trust only Him for the outcome.

Psalm 118:8, *It is better to trust in the LORD than to put confidence in man.*

Psalm 20:6-8, *Now know I that the LORD saveth his anointed; he will hear him from his holy heaven with the saving strength of his right hand. Some trust in chariots, and some in horses: but we will remember the name of the LORD our God. They are brought down and fallen: but we are risen, and stand upright. Save, LORD: let the king hear us when we call.*

- <u>Hopelessness - Feeling that it's too much to bear.</u>

1 Corinthians 10:13, *There hath no temptation taken you but such as in common to man; but God is faithful, who will not suffer you to be tempted above that ye are able; but will with the temptation also make a way to escape, that ye may be able to bear it.*

These are emotions that will give us a warped perspective. A person whose seed has been crushed sees every situation from a powerless position. A crushed seed is no different from a crushed spirit. It will render a person unfit for ministry. It takes away from your desire to want to become more. A person whose seed is crushed is not capable of encouraging others because they themselves feel discouraged. A crushed seed can be toxic to the body.

The Struggle is real, but so is our God!

- *Victorious*

We have the victory! We have already won! History has already been written!

Psalms 98:1, *O sing unto the Lord a new song; for he hath done marvellous things: his right hand, and his holy arm, hath gotten him the victory.*

James 1:2-3, *Consider it pure joy, my brothers and sisters, whenever you face trials of many kinds, because you know the testing of your faith produces perseverance.*

- *Overcomers*

Just as Christ has overcome death, hell and the grave. We too are overcomers in our trials, in our situations and through all our circumstances.

John 16:33, *These things I have spoken to you, so that in Me you may have peace in the world you have tribulation, but take courage: I have overcome the world.*

Romans 8:37, *But In all these things we overwhelmingly conquer through Him who loved us.*

- *Faithful*

God is a faithful God. He will never leave us or forsake us. Whatever the promise may be that we are being processed to handle, we are not alone. He is right in there with us.

Psalms 86:15, *But you, O Lord, are a God merciful and gracious, slow to anger and abounding in steadfast love and faithfulness.*

Deuteronomy 7:9, *Know therefore that the Lord your God is God, the faithful God who keeps covenant and steadfast love with those who love him and keep his commandments, to a thousand generations.*

There is pressure in the press!

2 Corinthians 4:7-9, *Now we have this treasure in jars of clay to show that this surpassingly great power is from God and not from us. We are pressed on all sides, but not crushed: perplexed, but not in despair; persecuted, but not forsaken; struck down, but not destroyed....*

Life's challenges bring pressures that we may feel we cannot handle, but because of this power that we have on the inside we will not be destroyed. We have to go through our process, but God will help us through it. When I think about the pressures we face when we are in the midst of trials, my attention is drawn to the wine press. A wine press is a device used to extract juice from crushed grapes during the wine making process!

There are a number of different styles of wine presses that are used by the wine maker, but their overall functionality is the same. Each style of press exerts controlled pressure in order to free the juice from the fruit (most often grapes). The pressure must be controlled especially with grapes, to avoid crushing the seeds and releasing a great deal of undesirable tannins into the wine. Tannins are a yellowish or brownish bitter-tasting organic substance present in the seed, the skin and the stem of the grape and when they are release heavily they can cause the wine to be very bitter and dis-tasteful.

Just like the crushing of the grapes produces wine. The pressures we are faced with when we endure them produce an anointing in our lives that is so sweet. They produce the oil we need to pour into others. God plants a seed in us and then He uses the pressures of life to nurture that seed. He uses those same pressures to cultivate the soil (which is us) to be able to provide and sustain a healthy environment for that seed to grow and mature. Just as the pressure is set and controlled by the wine maker, it is God who sets and controls the pressures of life. He knows just how much pressure to use. He uses just enough pressure to produce fruit in our lives, so we do not have to worry, God is never going to crush his seed! This is why we cannot give up in the process. We cannot let the pressures of life crush our seed and when we give up this is what happens.

God will never crush the seed, but it is us who can become so burdened and discouraged that we ourselves, crush our seed. When our seed is crushed we feel useless to the body of Christ and to the ministry. We do not feel we have anything to contribute but we miss the fact that this is just a part of our process.

Therefore, the word tells us we are pressed on all sides but we are not crushed. He is letting us know that no matter how tough the process may get there is a bright side to it all.

Everything gets tested in the process. Not only is God going to try your ministry in the process but He is going to try your character. He is going to try your lifestyle.

We cannot quit in the process because someone is depending on us to make it out. If we just hold on in our process God will give us renewed strength, where we feel depleted, He will restore us.

Isaiah 40:31, *But they that wait upon the LORD shall renew their strength; they shall mount up with wings as eagles; they shall run, and not be weary; and they shall walk, and not faint.*

"Wait patiently on the Lord!" This means that we are active and with expectancy doing those things that are in God's will that brings us closer to the promise. We will be tried. Our faith in what God has said and the promise He has made will be tested.

The enemy will sow any seed of doubt and unbelief to get you to abort the promise of God for your life. Do not quit in the process.

We are being formed as it relates to our character. Our character is built in the process and this is what God wants. He builds our character through the pressures of life and He builds our character through patience. He invested 13 years in building the character of Joseph!

The foundation of our character will determine the depth of our destination and the height of where God is taking us.

We will be prepared once we have put aside doubt and have allowed God the freedom to make the necessary changes to bring about His plan for us. The process is the trying season! It is where we wait and we fight!

Nuggets of Promise:

The process is where it seems we spend most of our time. Oftentimes, this is the place where we do not want to be, but it is necessary. While in jail Joseph asked the butler to get him released but if he had gotten an early release he would have aborted the deliverance of his entire family. It is not just about you! Someone else's deliverance and life is dependent on your going through your process. There is purpose in your process and it is bigger than you. It is all about the Kingdom of God. Sometimes God has to deny our cry for deliverance for the sake of others. Just know your crying is not in vain.

Finding purpose in the process!

We are made in the process. Our character is determined and defined through the process. How do we react under pressure? God is the potter and I am the clay (Jeremiah 18:1-6). This reference is to the nation of Israel, a chosen vessel to bring God's blessings to the world. We as individual believers are God's vessels (Acts 9:15, 2 Corinthians 4:7).

Pottery is clay that has been moulded, dried and fired usually with a glaze or finish, into a vessel or decorative object. So, before we are a vessel, we are clay. Clay is a natural product that is dug from the earth. It has decomposed from rock within the earth's crust. Clay bodies are mixed with additives that give the clay different properties when worked and fired. Clay can be moulded by hand or with the assistance of the potter's wheel. I would say God uses both when we are the clay. According to Isaiah 64:8, we are the workmanship of God's hand. Just the right amount of pressure by the hand of God determines how we turn out. We must yield to God's hand to be made useful. Clay must be fired to a temperature high enough to mature it (the heat of the process). The refining fire and the consuming fire.

What does this refining fire do?

Zechariah 13:9

And I will put this third into the fire, and refine them as one refines silver, and test them as gold is tested. They will call upon my name, and I will answer them. I will say, They are my people; and they will say, The Lord is my God.

1 Peter 1:7

So that the tested genuineness of your faith—more precious than gold that perishes though it is tested by fire—may be found to result in praise and glory and honour at the revelation of Jesus Christ.

Isaiah 48:10

Behold, I have refined you, but not as silver; I have tried you in the furnace of affliction.

What does the consuming fire do?

Hebrews 12:29

For our God is a consuming fire.

Deuteronomy 4:14

For the LORD thy God is a consuming fire, even a jealous God.

God burns out everything that is not like him. He gets rid of all the impurities that lie deep beneath the surface. The high temperature hardens the piece to enable it to hold water. We have to be able to hold the water of the word of God. There is purpose in the process. We are tried in the process by way of the Holy Spirit. By way of the tests and trials in our lives and it hardens us so that we can hold this living water. This is the word that He uses to water others.

Perhaps the greatest finish to our process of being made in the firing is the addition of liquid glaze to the surface of the unfired pot. It changes the chemical composition and fuzzes to the surface of the fired pot called vitreous- it can hold water. Sounds like the pot has been sealed!

Ephesians 1:13

In whom ye also trusted, after that ye heard the word of truth, the gospel of your salvation: in whom also after that ye believed, ye were sealed with that holy Spirit of promise,

Nuggets of Promise:

Do not run from the fire. It is in the fire that who and what you are in Christ is made a reality. The me inside of me, what the world needs to see, is made visible through the process. The fire burns away those things that are not needed to accomplish the will of God. God decides what we need and He decides we do not. Therefore, he sets the temperature accordingly. He sets the heat within the fire and He is always aware of how hot it is. He is in complete control!

Chapter Six
STUCK IN THE MIDDLE

When God speaks a word into our lives, it is a word of promise that points to our future. It is easy to want to immediately live in the reality of what has been promised. If only we can skip over everything we must do along the way and get to the promise! We have to be prepared for the things God has for us in order to maintain them once we have them. We have to be conditioned for that place He has for us to go and for those people He has for us to touch so that we are effective in the way He is calling us to be.

So, we hear the word and we imagine the promise, but we want no parts of the process. We shout over the prophecy and dance over the promise but we struggle through the process. There is an in-between stage and it is called the process. By the time we realize there is a process, we are already in it. We must recognize when we are in our process and then we must submit to it. It is hard to submit to something we do not understand or recognize for what it is. An un-discerned process feels exactly like an attack.

Therefore, we think it is the enemy. Once we feel uncomfortable changes taken place, we feel violated and go into fight mode, we get stuck fighting everything and everyone. We get stuck in the middle of the prophecy and the promise. Stuck in the middle of the word spoken and the thing that God has promised us.

When we realise the process is something we must let run its course. Then we will cease from all our futile thinking and trying to reason ourselves out of what will eventually cause us to become better. This is where we have to use the wisdom of God and inquire of Him what we should do? We must submit to the process of God for it is His will. There is a time for fighting, when we are contending for our faith which is in Jesus Christ but sometimes we must surrender and let God do a work in us that prepares us for something greater.

If we are to get through the process and make it to the promise, we have to be vulnerable to God. We have to allow Him to strip us of those things that will hinder us and keep us from our promise. We become stuck in the middle when we do not allow God to detox us. He must move some things out of the way. He has to first remove doubt and unbelief, because as soon as we hear the word, it is the enemy's job to steal it from us by causing us to doubt what was spoken.

When we are in our process, it seems like it is the longest season of our lives. We may feel like a prisoner of the process. It is all too easy to call a particular time in life, a season, but often times it is a prophetic process that God intends for us to go through. A prophetic process is a time in our life where we will experience a personal change from the inside out that is ordained of God and will produce an intended outcome. When we fight a prophetic process, we are fighting against the plan of God.

Nuggets of Promise:

Do not fight the process! When we fight against the process God has ordained for us to go through we add time to what seems like a sentence. Sometimes it may feel like the situation you are going through will never end, but if you just submit to the process God will get you there in record time.

Chapter Seven
PIECES OF THE PUZZLE

Prophecy will come at a time when you are dealing with challenges and situations that cause your perspective to be off. Sometimes things that are prophesied to you may not fit the current situation. Your perception could either cause every word to seem impossible or your perception through the eyes of faith can cause you to see yourself in the promise. In other words, it is whatever view you choose.

When God speaks a word into your life and you cannot conceive the promise of that word coming to pass, your perception is off. Remember God sees our end from our beginning. When He sends a prophecy, He is letting you in on one of the secrets of your life. If He speaks it, it shall come to pass. The only person that will prevent it from happening is you. Your faith or lack thereof will determine how much you will apply yourself in working towards this promise. God promises you a good job, with good benefits, great pay and even room for advancement. So, by faith you start researching jobs, update your resume and begin to start applying for positions. Our faith moves God on the word that He has already spoken to us.

It does not matter if it comes by way of reading His word, the pastor preaching, or a prophet prophesying, we need to always respond by faith which is an action word.   It takes faith to receive the word, because oftentimes our life will not look like the word that we have heard. When this happens, we must position ourselves to get what God has for us. It may seem strange for God to prophesy a wedding to someone who is not even dating. God sees further than we ever will and what He does allow us to see, we should consider it a blessing to be in the loop. Jesus Christ being human and divine did not know when He himself would return.

"But of that day and hour knoweth no man, no, not the angels of heaven, but my Father only (Matthew 24:36).*"*

My pastor taught me that everything we read and everything we hear through the word of God is downloaded and filed away within us. It may not make sense to us at the time, but when we need it He pulls it up to the surface. This was one of her many profound words that I have taken to heart. So, prophecy will not always make sense to us, but we can rest assure that every word has a purpose. We must grab God's words by faith and trust that He will not mislead us.

When the promise does not line up with our current reality (to us), we have to rely on faith and our trust in Him to help us to see what He sees. A prophetic word will seem outlandish to one whose situation is the direct opposite of what is being promised. When your life looks nothing like what God is speaking, you must defy all logic, shut down your feelings, and tell your mind to line up with the mind of Christ.

By faith great things have happened and it is this same faith that is needed in order to take hold of the word spoken over us and begin to walk and talk as though we believe it. God already knows the outcome. "He is not a man that He should lie." If He said it, it will come to pass. If He spoke it, it shall be. Close your eyes and see it by faith!

Nuggets of Promise:

Every piece fits. There are times when we hear from God and it seems so farfetched. Trust God, that piece fits somewhere in the puzzle. If you have ever done a puzzle with 100 pieces, it takes a while. You know what the puzzle should look like when finished, but you need to put every piece in its place. You have all the pieces you need, but you don't know exactly where each one belongs. This is something you will figure out over time. Every time you put another piece in, the picture becomes clearer to you. You may have some pieces right now that do not seem to fit into the plan of God for your life but sit it to the side for a bit and keep working. Soon you will find exactly where each piece belongs.

Chapter Eight
GOD SPEAKS A FULL PICTURE

The mind of God can never be gauged it can never be understood, accept He gives us the understanding. It is He who gives revelation to His thoughts, His plans and purpose for our lives.

Jeremiah 29:11, *For I know the thoughts that I think toward you, saith the LORD, thoughts of peace, and not of evil, to give you an expected end.*

When God speaks a word over your life, he speaks from the perspective of the outcome. He sees the conclusion of the matter and we are encouraged to look through the window of faith which causes us to trust that everything will be okay. Allowing God to lead us and following His direction in faith causes us to flow with the process and not fight it. God has a plan for us if we would only go with the flow.

Empty Vessels

Years ago, I was in my home town Toledo, Ohio at a women's retreat and I will never forget the speaker was a powerful woman of God from

Cleveland, Ohio by the name of Kimberly Williams. After she had spoken she began to go around the room and pour into all those God was leading her to. When she got to me she gave me a word about the widow's oil the scripture found in 2 Kings 4:1-7.

It states, *Now there cried a certain woman of the wives of the sons of the prophets unto Elisha, saying, Thy servant my husband is dead; and thou knowest that thy servant did fear the LORD: and the creditor is come to take unto him my two sons to be bondmen. And Elisha said unto her, What shall I do for thee? tell me, what hast thou in the house? And she said, Thine handmaid hath not anything in the house, save a pot of oil. Then he said, Go, borrow thee vessels abroad of all thy neighbours, even empty vessels; borrow not a few. And when thou art come in, thou shalt shut the door upon thee and upon thy sons, and shalt pour out into all those vessels, and thou shalt set aside that which is full. So, she went from him, and shut the door upon her and upon her sons, who brought the vessels to her; and she poured out. And it came to pass, when the vessels were full, that she said unto her son, Bring me yet a vessel. And he said unto her, There is not a vessel more. And the oil stayed. Then she came and told the man of God. And he said, Go, sell the oil, and pay thy debt, and live thou and thy children of the rest.*

When a person prophesies the word of God over your life, the Spirit of God in you should be able to bear witness to what is being said. So, I received this word and I immediately began think of a project I had begun to work on within my business. At this time, I had not become a salon owner but was working as an independent contractor at someone else's salon.

However, when I heard the word, in my mind it all made sense. So, I went years thinking I knew what this word meant and feeling as though I needed to complete this project and the prophecy would be fulfilled. It was over 12 years ago when I received this word.

According to Isaiah 55:8, *For my thoughts are not your thoughts, neither are your ways my ways, saith the LORD.*

Even when we put on the mind of Christ as it helps us to think "like" him and it causes our character to be more like his, we still cannot fully see the whole picture. So, fast forward to the present, I'm sitting in church one Sunday in April 2017, and my pastor Bishop Pat McKinstry, is preaching and she shared with us, there was a time early in her ministry when she prayed for God to fill the church with people and He spoke to her and said the people are the church, you fill them with me.

That thing resonated in me so, I had to share with my Bishop, how I had been praying for God to fill my business with clients and employees. I had promised Him if He sent the people I would fill them with Him. I would share His word and His goodness and if they needed prayer I would give them that too. Now this was nothing new, it was always something I had done especially once I had opened my own business in 2005 but I had not realized just how much this was to become a staple in my business.

My business was built on the foundation of a promise God gave to me when I graduated high school with my Cosmetology licence in 1989. He told me all those years ago that I would own my own business one day. Back to the revelation, I still had not caught the full meaning. It wasn't until May 18th of 2017 at 7:59am that I received the full revelation. The project although it would become useful to the structure of my business, was only a very small almost insignificant piece of the puzzle. So, I'm talking to this same woman who had prophesied to me all those years prior and she began to pray for me and my business and its success. Now, she had become my Business Advisor, and had helped me negotiate the deal for the expansion of my business and had continued to offer her support with anything I needed as it pertained the business.

I was on the phone with her early in the morning and she began to pray. After she prayed we gave glory and honour to God and she told me that I needed empty vessels. I needed people who I would be able to shape and mold into what I needed them to be. I need empty vessels I can pour into, those who would understand the vision I have for my business and run with it. God would supply the people and I would fill them with Him.

See this thing was bigger than any business, bigger than doing hair. There are salons on almost every corner and an abundance of hairstylist who do amazing work. It is bigger than that. Can I be that entrepreneur and work with that group of people that when clients come to my establishment they know it is different? Can people come to my salon and feel different from the inside out? Can they come in and leave out never being the same again?

This place that God gave me was a place He set apart, not only to beautify a person on the outside, but to tap into their inner man. A place where they can be filled if they so choose to be. It was a place that was designed for ministry and a place where they could be introduced to Him.

In the scripture, the widow was told to borrow vessels. Not one- person God sends through my establishment belongs to me. They are borrowed vessels that I am to fill with the precious oil, the anointing of God. I am to fill them with His word, allow them to sit in his presence and pray for them if I see the need. Those that come in who know the Lord for themselves are there to touch and agree but for those who come in who do not know Him, now have a chance to receive Christ right there in the hair salon.

Not only has God blessed and anointed my hands for prosperity but also to be able to bless His people. The oil that flowed for the widow and her sons did not stop flowing until there were no more vessels. God will supply! As long as there is a need, as long as there is an empty vessel he will pour out of Himself. I am a vessel being used by God to fill other vessels.

1 Corinthians 15:46

Howbeit that was not first which is spiritual, but that which is natural; and afterward that which is spiritual.

First natural then spiritual.

God sets us up in the natural so that we can begin to operate spiritually.

2 sides to the vision.

There is a natural side and there is a spiritual side to the vision.

The natural side to the vision God gave me for my business was my product line. Fill the bottles/empty vessels with products, retail them, earn profit/ increase, pay debt and live off the rest. This would be my retirement package.

Spiritual side: Empty vessels as people, fill them and help build the kingdom. This is the greater purpose in seeing the vision fulfilled.

Platform for ministry! I learned a long time ago that my work behind the chair was less about the hairstyles and more about pouring into people. I have been amazed at how much people just need to be heard. As a stylist, I have had the pleasure of being a listening ear to many of my clients who trust me and think enough of me to share their lives with me. I get to hear about birthdays, anniversaries, engagements, children, relationships, jobs etc. I also get to comfort my clients when they deal with loss or tragedy and the best part about it is I get to comfort them with the word and the love of Christ.

He gives me what to say to let that person know that He hears them and is there for them. Oftentimes, I am asked to pray for the individual and it gives me great joy to do so. My job is not just a job but most importantly it is a platform for ministry. Yes, I have been called to preach the word of God according to Luke 4:18, *The Spirit of the Lord is upon me, because he hath anointed me to preach the gospel to the poor; he hath sent me to heal the broken-hearted, to preach deliverance to the captives, and recovering of sight to the blind, to set at liberty them that are bruised,* but aren't we all ministers? If I never get behind a pulpit again, I am still called to minister the word of God.

God makes opportunities for us to minister to others, about His goodness and His grace. Many times, I have wondered why people have shared with me some of their most intimate details of their life. However, I know God allows us to make divine connections when He wants to send His word into the life of another.

Filled Vessels:

2 Corinthians 4:7, *But we have this treasure in earthen vessels, that the excellency of the power may be of God, and not of us.*

This was Jesus' life's work. He fills us with His Spirit so that we can fill others. He shares pieces of Himself to help us to become more like Him. This is His ministry, the ministry of reconciliation. It is not just His, but it belongs to us too!

Prophecy   *Process*   *Promise*

2 Corinthians 5:17-19, *Therefore, if anyone is in Christ, he is a new creation. The old has passed away; behold, the new has come. All this is from God, who reconciled us to himself through Christ and gave us the ministry of reconciliation; that God was reconciling the world to himself in Christ, not counting men's trespasses against them, and he has committed to us the message of reconciliation.*

Nuggets of Promise:

When God speaks to us, He speaks the whole conclusion of the matter. Do not let your inability to see what God sees cause you to stagger at the promise. Do not let it cause you to disbelieve the promise God has spoken. On the strength of who God is, believe anyhow. Believe it! Step out on faith! Go after what He says you can have, be and do, because He said so!

Chapter Nine
MAKING ENDS MEET

Once I hear the word which speaks of the promise I immediately in my mind, join the two together. However, when I try to do this in the natural God says, no and He places me in the middle of the two. Now, I am standing in my process. I am stuck in the middle of my prophecy and my promise. I am trying to reconcile the prophecy to the promise! I used the word reconcile, because to God it is already together, but it comes to us in pieces. We get the word and how it relates to the promise but what we do not consider is the process! What is it going to take! I have got a tight grip with one hand on the prophecy and the other is on my promise! At times, it may feel like you are being split in two but hold on anyway! It might be a struggle but hold on.

It might be hard, but hold on do not give up because you have got to make it to your promise! You have got to say to yourself, "I cannot let go of the prophecy until I see the promise come to pass!" Our process has to happen! It is in the process that God gives us the ability handle the promise!

In the process, we are processed:

- We are matured
- We learn patience
- Where we are weak we are made strong
- We are taught to say what God says
- We are taught to pray God's word
- We learn the importance of obedience
- We make sacrifices
- We fight for our faith
- Our faith increases
- We are established
- We trust God more
- We are trained to hear and follow God's voice
- We receive revelation from Him
- We realize it is not all about us
- We see the bigger picture
- We look forward to the promise
- We learn how to get the victory
- We come out with victory
- We walk into our promise

Nuggets of Promise:

There will be things in our lives that God will speak and we will not have to do a single thing to see it happen. This is an unconditional promise. Then there are promises He has made that will require us to be processed so that we are able to handle what's coming. On one end, we have the prophecy, and on the other we have the promise. Consider all that you must do, and all you must allow God to do through you in order to make the two ends meet. You have to be a willing participant and you have to know that God is able to do just what He has promised. He can and He will make ends meet!

The Timing of The Prophecy of God

Sometimes, we have waited so long for the manifestation of the promise that we begin to get discouraged. We begin to wonder is it really going to happen. To shield ourselves from any more pain we may even tell God, if it is not Your will for me, then please take this desire away. This is not a healthy way to deal with waiting on our promise.

Psalm 37:1-4, *Fret not thyself because of evildoers, neither be thou envious against the workers of iniquity. For they shall soon be cut down like the grass, and wither as the green herb. Trust in the Lord and do good; so shalt thou dwell in the land, and verily thou shall be fed. Delight thyself also in the Lord; and he shall and he shall give thee the desires of thine heart.*

When God speaks a word in our lives, it may not come to pass for some time. It does not mean the word was out of season, it is just that we have to be processed in order to receive what He has for us. He has a specific time for that word or promise to be made manifest.

Ecclesiastes 3:3, *To everything there is a season, and a time to every purpose under the heaven:*

Not only do we have to wait on the promise but we have to do something while we are in our process. We have to allow God to condition us so that we are mentally, spiritually and even physically able to carry the promise once He gives it to us. It is like being in an incubation period. An incubation period is the time that begins with us hearing the word that speaks of the promise to the time we begin to see a thing manifested.

It is all a part of the process. We have to trust the timing of God and not our own deadlines and perceived time lines. God is not limited by space and time. One of the greatest challenges in waiting on prophecy to be fulfilled is watching what we say. We have to consistently speak the promise while we are walking through the process. "God spoke, God Spoke, God Spoke and then God saw!" (Dr. Pat McKinstry). God has given us this same creative power. When we speak we have great influence over our situations, over circumstances and over our lives. We have to watch how we speak while in our process.

The Maxwell leadership Bible list four functions of the tongue:

1. The tongue as a gauge.

Our tongue helps us to gauge how mature we are. Our faith will never gauge higher than our words.

James 3:1-2 *Not many of you should become teachers, my brothers, because you know that we who teach will be judged more strictly.*

We all stumble in many ways. If anyone is never at fault in what he says, he is a perfect man, able to control his whole body....

2. To Guide.

If we can control our tongue we can dictate the direction of our lives.

James 3:3-5, *Behold, we put bits in the horses' mouths, that they may obey us; and we turn about their whole body. Behold also the ships, which though they be so great, and are driven of fierce winds, yet are they turned about with a very small helm, whithersoever the governor listeth. Even so the tongue is a little member, and boasteth great things. Behold, how great a matter a little fire kindleth!*

3. To Gird.

There is great power in the tongue. This power is meant to send us down the right path.

James 6:8, *And the tongue is a fire, a world of iniquity: so is the tongue among our members, that it defileth the whole body, and setteth on fire the course of nature; and it is set on fire of hell. For every kind of beasts, and of birds, and of serpents, and of things in the sea, is tamed, and hath been tamed of mankind: But the tongue can no man tame; it is an unruly evil, full of deadly poison.*

4. To Guard.

A good tongue protects our integrity. We've had the greatest example of a tamed tongue in the journey of Jesus to the cross.

James 3:9-18, *Therewith bless we God, even the Father; and therewith curse we men, which are made after the similitude of God. Out of the same mouth proceedeth blessing and cursing. My brethren, these things ought not so to be. Doth a fountain send forth at the same place sweet water and bitter? Can the fig tree, my brethren, bear olive berries? either a vine, figs? so can no fountain both yield salt water and fresh. Who is a wise man and endued with knowledge among you? let him shew out of a good conversation his works with meekness of wisdom.*

But if ye have bitter envying and strife in your hearts, glory not, and lie not against the truth. This wisdom descendeth not from above, but is earthly, sensual, devilish. For where envying and strife is, there is confusion and every evil work. But the wisdom that is from above is first pure, then peaceable, gentle, and easy to be intreated, full of mercy and good fruits, without partiality, and without hypocrisy. And the fruit of righteousness is sown in peace of them that make peace.

"He was oppressed, and he was afflicted, yet he opened not his mouth: he is brought as a lamb to

the slaughter, and as a sheep before her shearers is dumb, so he openeth not his mouth (Isaiah 53:7)."

Jesus never said a word. We cannot suffer a stubbed toe, but He suffered torture, beating and death without a word. He did not complain. He did not talk about how unfair it was, how innocent he was or how long all this was taking. This was the greatest example of perfect patience. We will see our promise if we just have patience in the process.

What gets us through the process?

Patience

We cannot rush the process. Does the baker leave out an ingredient in baking a cake or cut the timer 15 minutes short? That cake would be un-done and so will our promise. We will not mature enough to handle the promise of God if we do not complete the process.

James 1:4, *But let patience have her perfect work, that ye may be perfect and entire, wanting nothing.*

Isaiah 40:31, *But they that wait upon the Lord shall renew their strength; they shall mount up with wings as eagles; they shall run, and not be weary; and they shall walk and not faint.*

Persistence

Giving up is not an option! We must keep at it until we finish. Surely, we will never see the promise if we quit.

Galatians 6:9, *And let us not grow weary of doing good, for in due season we will reap, if we do not give up.*

Matthew 7:7, *Ask, and it shall be given you; seek, and ye shall find; knock, and it shall be opened unto you:*

Peace

Do not panic, call on the peace of God to help you stay calm and remain focused. Anxiety is just a distraction and it opens the door for fear.

1 Peter 5:7, *Cast all your anxiety on Him because He cares for yourself*

Isaiah 26:3, *You will keep him in perfect peace, whose mind is stayed on You, because he trusts in You.*

Prayer

Prayer is always the key. Talk to God and let God speak to you. It is in our communing with Him that we find direction.

1 Thessalonians 5:17, *Pray without ceasing,*

Colossians 4:2, *Continue steadfastly in prayer, being watchful in it with thanksgiving.*

Power

We must rely on the power of God, it is by this same power that He has done miraculous things. It is ours and we must draw from it.

Philippians 4:13, *I can do all things through Christ who strengthens me.*

2 Timothy 1:7, *For God has not given us a spirit of fear, but of power and of love and of a sound mind.*

Praise

It is our praise that will get us through the process. No matter what we are facing praise God through it all and confound the enemy.

James 5:13, *Is anyone among you suffering? Let him pray. Is anyone cheerful? Let him sing praise.*

2 Corinthians 1:3-4, *Praise be to the God and Father of our Lord Jesus Christ, the Father of compassion and the God of all comfort, who comforts us in all our troubles, so that we can comfort those in any trouble with the comfort we ourselves receive from God.*

Chapter Ten
THE UNIVERSAL PROMISE

God's announcement of His plan of salvation and blessing of His people is the ultimate promise. A promise embraces both the declaration and deed. God's promise begins with a declaration made by Him. It covers His future plan, not only for one race but for all nations of the earth. Jesus is the greatest teacher that ever was when it comes to the process. I often joke about having a straight-ahead ministry, one in which I am so focused on God and what he has me doing that I will not engage in anything that will get me off track. I have now realized throughout my own journey that I have to possess a straight-ahead ministry.

Isaiah 50:7, *For the Lord God will help me; therefore, shall I not be confounded; therefore, have I set my face like flint, and I know that I will not be ashamed.*

In my process, I have had to set my face like flint. Flint is a figure of hardness in Isaiah 50:7 and Ezekiel 3:9. Flint used here means, the Messiah would be firm and resolute amidst all contempt and scorn which He would meet; that He had made up in His mind to endure it and would not shrink from any kind of degree of suffering which would be necessary to accomplish the great work in which He was engaged. There is no greater example for us to follow. I have set my face like flint while I am going through my process. I will be firm and resolute in the midst of everything, the contempt, the scorn, the trials and the testing. I will not shrink back from that which I have to endure to get to my promise. Whatever degree of suffering I must endure, I know that if I set my face like stone, I shall not be moved.

Through all our suffering and even our trials it's easy for others to look and assume that we are the cause and what we are dealing with is a direct result of our own actions. There are times that this is the case and then there are times when it's not. Sometimes it's just the process we may have to go through to get to where God is taking us. Jesus did nothing wrong. He was the sacrifice for all that humanity has done, for all our sins and griefs. He suffered knowing He had done nothing and He set his face like a flint. He did not let the scorn and the shame or anger distract Him. He did not allow it to break Him nor did he allow it to cause Him to abort the mission. When we are positioned in our process it may seem like mission impossible, but as long as we stay focused we will finish.   God wants to accomplish some great things through us and all that we go through. It may not be easy and it may not feel good but our promise is at the finish line.

Nuggets of Promise:

The Universal promise of salvation is free to every one of us, but just because something is free does not mean it will not cost us. Jesus paid with His life so that we can have a chance to receive eternal life. There is a chance some will take it and perhaps some will not, but for those who choose salvation, it comes at a price. We have nothing to lose and everything to gain by just saying, yes! What are you willing to sacrifice?

Chapter Eleven
MANIFESTED MIRACLES

Our process prepares us and puts us in position to possess the promise. We go through our process not just for us but for our loved ones and those connected to us. There are some things God promised us and some people He has declared to belong to the Kingdom. This is why we have to endure the process. There are people that are watching us go through waiting on us to fail so they can declare that they knew all along that God is not real in our lives, but they have to stay tuned to the end. God is going to show up in a miraculous way.

When we feel like giving up we must hold on to the promise. We have to envision all the people He promised to save, those He promised to deliver and those He promised to set free and we have to see them coming out. When we think of miracles we think of these things. We see the blind being made to see, the lame being made to walk and dumb being made to talk. We see people getting out of hospital beds, out of wheelchairs and even off of morgue tables. We see people's lives being spared from near death experiences and all kinds of sickness and disease. There are miracles waiting to manifest with the promise of God! Jesus has done, is doing and will do all of these things and He expects us to do them as well. Whole nations were saved from destruction, families were spared from famine all because someone chose to stay in their process.

It may feel like we are in the hot seat and we are, but there is so much at stake. If we could not bare it, God would not have chosen us. While we are in our process, God is perfecting those things that concern us. Hallelujah! That deserves a praise right there! Our God is taking care of it all.

Nuggets of Promise:

If you want to see miracles happen in your life, you must yield to the voice and the Spirit of God. Be used of Him. Let His will be done in your life. Listen to the Holy Spirit and let Him guide you into all truth.

APPENDIX A

The Blueprint...

The process that we go through to achieve what God has spoken is tailor made for us. We are the only one who can endure the process that He has ordained for our lives. This process is the blueprint of our promise and we must complete it, in order to get to our destiny.

APPENDIX B

Taking Back Your Power!

This book is to be used as a tool to help believers and non-believers who may be struggling through the process that leads them to their promise. It will open their eyes to the pitfalls in the process and help them to push their way through to the other side. We must accept that the greatest work God wants to do is sometimes on the inside of us and we have to submit to the process and let Him have His way. We take back our power to overcome when we submit to the power and Spirit of God.

CONCLUSION

When we say, yes to God we say, yes to the process, we say, yes to the process in which we walk out our salvation. Also, we say, yes to the process laid before any of the things He has promised us. Reaching our destiny depends on how we progress, how we are changed and how we meet the challenges of our process. It will not be easy and it will not move according to our timeline. It is ordained by God and we have to take every step of it.

Wanda R. Presberry

ABOUT THE AUTHOR

Wanda Presberry is a called and ordained Elder of the Gospel of Christ. She is a profound teacher of the word of God, and has a passion for sharing the word with others. Early in her ministry she has taught Bible Study, Sunday school, preached Sunday services, and have been called on to teach at women's retreats. She currently teaches Sunday School for youth ages 13 to 17 years old. Her passion is to reach young girls and women who have been faced with difficult situations, and those who need to know that through the love of Christ they can overcome anything in this life. She has earned a Bachelor of Theology from McKinstry Midwest College of Theology, a Bachelor of Leadership from Ohio Christian University, and a Master's Degree in Pastoral Care and Counselling from Ohio Christian University. Her primary focus is to pour Christ into the lives of others and to see women, men, girls and boys changed for Christ everywhere.

REFERENCES

Holman Illustrated Bible Dictionary (2003). Nashville, TN: Holman Bible Publishers

The Holy Bible (Sixth Ed.). (2015). Peabody, MA: Hendrickson Publishers Marketing.

Maxwell, J. C. (2002). The Maxwell Leadership Bible